BIRDS NOBODY LOVES

A Book of Vultures & Grackles

by

James Brush

Coyote Mercury Press
Austin, TX

For Silas & Rachel

Birds Nobody Loves: A Book of Vultures & Grackles

Published by Coyote Mercury Press
Austin, TX

ISBN 978-0-9849205-0-1

Contents

While Sitting in Church

I didn't hear a word the priest said,
but I saw the vultures circling

rising

in the air above the lake
outside the windows
beyond the altar.

Things looked clearer out there,
and it made perfect sense to see

God skipping church that day
just to ride thermals with the angels.

Confession

(I caught my breath

when you confessed

that you love vultures too.)

Patton's Army

A scene in *Patton*. Fallen infantrymen.
Buzzards pick over bodies.

A soldier with a machine gun
shoots the birds. I cheer;
my mom scolds me.

Those birds aren't doing anything wrong.

Now I understand
vultures, too, are beautiful:
they clean our messes

faster than military undertakers
or even the highway department.

Quiscalus Mexicanus

1.
Anglicized his name to honor his great tail
and flew north over the border walls.

Some like to say his tail is boat-like, confusing
him with his shore-hugging cousins, but his

eyes glitter brighter and he stays inland,
staking claims to town squares on the plains

where his strange and wild music clashes
with the traditions of more established birds.

2.
The car radio blares louder than the wind, louder
than the grackles chattering in the city trees.

*Grackles are socialists. They weren't born in the U.S. Grackles
do what Hitler did. Shouldn't even call 'em passerines; they're
not even birds. Sub-birds at best. They're antichrists or at
least lesser demons. They're plotting the reconquista! Listen!
They're out there, the ugly filthy things!*

We turn it off.

3.
High on a power line, he cranes his neck upward
stretching his beak to drink this northern sky.

On other power lines, other grackles do the same,
each hungry to gulp down this bright blue day.

On March 1st

the grackles opened
like gates in the trees
shadow birds, eyes glistening
you could almost imagine
these noisy shades
abandoning tangible birds,
parking lots and steel dumpsters
in their odyssey through
suburban woods,
clacking and creaking
like machines or clocks
ticking away the last
hoarse seconds of winter.

Good Authority

I always thought they'd like death metal,
but I've got it on good authority
vultures prefer smooth jazz.

Ambulance rides can be rough;
vultures know this and relax.
Watching the highway, they know
everyone gets his turn.

Turkey vultures can smell a corpse
from hundreds of feet up. Outflying
Cessnas they arrive first on the scene.

Black vultures follow, pushing
solitary turkeys to the rotting edges.

The black vultures brag that by traveling
together they've learned to attack and kill
small animals: calves and possums.

Straightening their ties, they discuss
elaborate plans to go public. Someday,
they claim, they will become hawks or eagles.

The turkey vulture listens to this talk,
wondering if he too will evolve.

Grackle Ghazal

I stroll the streets and dodge mangy grackles,
fluttering birds in trees, those angry grackles.

Black feet and dark beaks snap at my sandwich—
I'm surrounded by the grabby grackles!

I sit a bench and study pawns and queens
'til "checkmate's" called by the cagey grackles.

At dinner parties, I near drop my drink
shocked by the sins of the feisty grackles.

I hang for hours on back porches, strumming
old guitars, swapping lies with folksy grackles.

At night, I roost in city trees and sing
wild croaking songs, toasting jolly grackles.

Circling Vultures

1.
We drove out of Colorado Bend,
passed a dead tree full of vultures.
It was hard to imagine anything
more perfect for a Texas morning.
That day, we believed in forever,
even as we passed the vulture tree.

2.
Along the highways, vultures soar overhead,
shadows sharing asphalt with cars that run down
those shadows unnoticed by the drivers.
The vultures don't miss anything.
They know we'll be back this way.
They will wait, and in the meantime,
their wings will barely move.

3.
One time I saw a vulture with a secondary feather
bent backwards and up like the flap on an
airplane's wing as it comes in for a landing.
The bird didn't seem to mind his twisted feather,
and when I saw him again,
he was 15 miles down the road,
and I was on my way home.

4.
I asked a birder if he'd seen anything interesting.
He spat on the ground, saliva sizzling on summer
pavement. *Nothing. Just a bunch of buzzards.*
The vultures ignored us and our binoculars, content
to trace their simple prophecy in the sky.

The Grackle Tree

After a few days under the grackle tree, the blue sedan began to develop a white pox, which spread with each passing night. The automedics shook their heads in grim certainty, fully aware of the limits of their training and skill. Eventually, it was decided that the problem was environmental, and men with shotguns came and took determined aim into the trees before firing blanks into the upper boughs. Sometimes the grackles would scatter at the sound, flying off to local birdbaths where they would clean up before returning to their usual roost. The men, satisfied, moved down the street where they would take shots at the starling tree, pigeon tree, and a supposed second grackle tree that legend had it was located somewhere south of 16th Street. Despite the diligence of the men, the grackles always returned, and the slow infection of the blue sedan continued. After a month, no one remembered what color the car had been, and no one ever discussed its owners or what became of them.

grackle tree
boughs shake and chatter
at the cars

Chasing Westward

The vultures are heading west, their slow flying
shadow grace just an illusion of the blank sky.

Clock them. They're racing away fast as thought.
Faster than often-repeated certainties and fears.

They escape with gizzards full, hurtling toward the sun,
shuttling some soul's nourishing remains westward.

Out there, I hope, they'll catch the day that never ends,
the place, I believe, night will never fall.

After sunset, I hear the rumbling highway, cars
chasing westward, chasing dreams, the fading light.

Winter Solstice

Grackles poke around the right-of-way,
a confusion of iridescent-robed seekers,
an endless search for grass seeds.

The junkie at the intersection watches,
never takes his eyes off the grackles
even when I hand him some crackers
and dried bits of bread. I look in his eyes,

nobody's home, and we both understand
the grackles' bright yellow eyes are more alive,
more aware of the gray curtain coming down
fast from the north. He stretches his arms

ready to ride that icy tailwind south, but the
light changes to green—too many cars now
block his path, but it's useless anyway.

All his flight feathers fell out six years ago.

He stands in exhaust fumes, praying that
grackles share seed when snow's coming.

Summer Solstice

Three o'clock in the afternoon,
central Texas summer day,
over a hundred degrees out.
I know there will be no birds,
nothing but grackles and vultures.
I go out, and I'm not surprised.
Only common grackles like this heat.
The other birds hold still like
knots in the trees, silent waiting for dusk,
trying to keep their colors from melting
into the brown grass and faded leaves.
Overhead turkey vultures soar
on steady outstretched wings,
folding sky and letting it move
around and over them as they ride
thermals up to more temperate
atmospheric zones. Meanwhile,
the grackles and I enjoy the heat
until the other birds begin to stir
and it's time for me to go home.

Greyhound Joey vs. the Grackle

Three bites taken on the run, two soggy feathers
float from his mouth, no sign left of any bird.

I call animal emergency:
Yuck, but your dog will be fine.
It's what he's made to do.

I call another vet just to be sure.
First, *Ewww.* But I am told the same.

It's what he's made to do.

My friends weigh in:
What's one less grackle?
I hate those filthy birds.
Thank goodness. Grackles are awful.

Now, each morning I fill the feeders
as I've always done, and Joey follows
as he always has, but something's new:

in the way he watches me pour the seed,
he admires how the trapper baits his traps.

An Avicentric Model

I watch a
vulture

soar in perfect
stillness

across
open sky.

::

Or is it me
moving,

stuck to
earth,

rotating beneath
fixed birds?

::

Do I know the
math

to make this
true?

If I did,
would you believe?

Creed for Cathartes Aura

We shit on our own feet,
try anything to be cool.

We seek death out;
so we can live and grow.

We circle tragedy, hope
to steal something from it.

We wobble when soaring;
balance requires adjustment.

We draw circles between clouds,
and patrol the land beneath.

We live in a world of cycles;
We give carrion new life.

In the Time of the Automobile

Deer run thick along our road;
they don't even think about the cars.

Vultures fly thick above our road;
they know all about the cars and wait.

At night, they hiss from the trees, grunting
tales about all the cars that stopped in time.

The deer don't usually remember.
They forget to fear the cars, so unlike
discriminating mountain lions and wolves,
forgotten now despite genetic warnings.

The vultures watch the cars approach,
watch the deer stand still or sometimes
whisper, *Run*, just a moment too late.

Though I hate to see the ruined bodies,
I don't begrudge the vultures' venison;
their meals must be pretty tasty to them
and besides (I admit it) I sometimes find

I'm fascinated by the morning meetings
around their roadside meals.

A Cackle of Grackles

mostly grackles—
unoiled hinges creaking
high in the trees.

—

strutting, beak open,
a grackle displays his wings
the female decides.

—

a tornado of grackles
swirls through the lot
leaving a sparrow

—

grackles spill across the sky:
lap lanes leading to the sun.

I adjust my backstroke
                    and follow.

a pair of grackles
nuk-nuking to the moon
heat-silent street

—

reeds bend
the weight of grackles
chattering

—

a flock of grackles
barges into the live oaks
acorns thunk rooftops

—

the gates of spring
creak open
a jay tilts his head

grackles return
shadows descend

A Committee of Vultures

a pair of black vultures
sits on the neighbor's rooftop
wings open to the sun

—

shadows
across a brown field
vultures   searching

—

far beyond the swallows
vultures haunt thermals
silent and endless

—

on a bed of leaves,
a deer skeleton picked clean,
save one furry hoof

in a cloudless sky
a vulture circles the prairie
seeking an ending

—

pale sky
two vultures
wheel upward

slow steady
wingbeats

—

a soaring vulture
his graceful arc
pierced
by fighter planes
the color of sky

—

a black vulture rides
down the cold front wind
new year's eve

My Tourist Yard

They show up in April with the cowbirds
and the red wings, all the icterids returning.

By June they're hoarding the feeders,
the birdbaths and the lawn, clucking

in the trees and teaching their young.
By August they've returned to the parking lot

at the grocery store, handing the keys to the yard
back to the chickadees and titmice who,

more deferential, somehow seem a little
sweeter than their noisy cousins who only

summer here, throw their cash around and
leave without learning the culture or our ways.

God Hates Grackles

They drove down from some mega church in Kansas with signs reading, "God hates grackles," and "Grackles spread disease & crap on everything." One little girl with blond pigtails tied with blue ribbons carried a sign saying, "No more icky turds." They marched up and down the street outside the capitol chanting verses from Leviticus about unclean birds, occasionally stopping to extol the virtues of godly American fried chicken and turkey club sandwiches. From their trees, the grackles watched with little interest. They heard the repetitive nuk-nuk-nuk of the chanters and wondered at the rusty-hinge noises they made on the street below but mostly, they preened their shiny purple feathers and craned their necks toward the open sky above.

This went on for most of the afternoon and as the heat increased, the protesters grew more desperate, more willing to go beyond the veil of free speech. One man cast a stone. There was a moment's pause as the world waited for the grackles to craft a response. Seconds grew to minutes, and the protesters glanced at one another, nervous, waiting. Suddenly all the grackles exploded skyward in a storm of wings and wild hallelujahs. The protesters watched with squinted eyes as the birds flew ever higher, each beat of their dark wings carrying them deeper into the sky and closer to God than anyone on the street below could imagine.

Blinded by the summer sky into which the grackles had disappeared, the protesters fumbled for their signs, packed them back on the bus, cursing the ugly grackles for their filthy ways and for not being blue birds or cardinals. Resentful and secretly wishing they too had wings and beautiful iridescent plumage, they drove back north, never once leaving the ground.

Trembling

wings
tremble

cold front
falls gray from
northern skies

dry fields ripple—
summer's grass
dead and brown
hides nothing

not even shadows
from the vulture
spiraling lower

waiting
waiting

for something
to freeze

Say Grackle

Purple iridescence,
        a hard-edged thrill to say.

How can a person not love
        the chance to repeat the word:

                grackle?

I'll never understand
        why everyone hates grackles.

(But then I don't have
        thousands living in my trees.)

Outside my window,
        a fledgling takes food:

an adult teaches
        the young bird how to live.

I'll lose a whole day
        watching, wishing them well.

Grackle,
        grackle, grackle.

Lines Discovered in an Aging Ornithologist's Field Journal

When the end comes, don't
plant me in the ground, trapped
in just one piece of earth.

Why not leave me by
the highway for the vultures
and maybe for the crows
who will take my unseeing eyes.

Then, at last, I could soar,
finally fly on dusky wings
outstretched,

buried in the sky.

Optimist

Whisper:
a vulture's wings—
I keep going

Notes

About the birds in this book: Vultures are large carrion-eating birds. The turkey vulture (*Cathartes aura*) and black vulture (*Coragyps atratus*) are native to the Americas and common in parts of the United States. True grackles are a blackbird-like species also native to the Americas. The common grackle (*Quiscalus quiscula*) and great-tailed grackle (*Quiscalus mexicanus*) are those most frequently seen in the US.

"Quiscalus Mexicanus": The great-tailed grackle is in the midst of a century-long range expansion into the western US.

"Good Authority": Black vultures have been observed working together to kill small animals. Turkey vultures can locate carcasses by smell. Black vultures often follow turkey vultures to food.

"Creed for Cathartes Aura": Vultures defecate on their own feet, possibly to stay cool in the summertime.

List of Illustrations

Common grackle: pages 13, 21, 30, 34
Great-tailed grackle: cover & page 8
Turkey vulture: pages 4, 16, 37, 39, 40, & back cover
Black vulture: title page & page 25

All illustrations by the author
Author photo by Rachel Brush

Acknowledgements

My thanks to the editors of the following journals for first publishing some of these poems:

Bolts of Silk: "My Tourist Yard" and "Good Authority"

Thirteen Myna Birds: "God Hates Grackles," "Lines Discovered in an Aging Ornithologist's Field Journal," and "Circling Vultures"

a handful of stones: "grackles spill across the sky"

Four and Twenty: "Optimist"

tinywords: "on a bed of leaves"

Houston Literary Review: "Greyhound Joey vs. the Grackle"

Pay Attention: A River of Stones Anthology: "pale sky"

Nothing. No One. Nowhere: "The Grackle Tree"

qarrtsiluni: "While Sitting in Church" (Videopoem)

Curio Poetry: "Winter Solstice" and "In the Time of the Automobile"

Many of these poems first appeared on one or the other of my blogs, *Coyote Mercury* and *a gnarled oak*, so my thanks to those readers who left kind and encouraging comments, particularly Deb Scott and Rachel Brush who gave invaluable feedback on the manuscript.

About the Author

James Brush is a high school English teacher. He published his first novel, *A Place Without a Postcard*, in 2003. His poems have appeared in various journals online and in print, and he keeps a full list of publications at his blog *Coyote Mercury*. He really does like vultures and grackles, which is lucky since he lives in central Texas.

You can find James online at any of the following places:

Coyote Mercury (his personal blog): coyotemercury.com
a gnarled oak (his mirco-poetry blog): gnarledoak.org
Twitter: twitter.com/jdbrush

Made in the USA
Coppell, TX
06 December 2020